BRITISH RAILWAYS STEAMING THROUGH THE SIXTIES

Volume Four

Compiled by
PETER HANDS & COLIN RICHARDS

DEFIANT PUBLICATIONS
190 Yoxall Road, Shirley
Solihull, West Midlands.

Printed in the United Kingdom by Netherwood Dalton & Co Ltd, Huddersfield, England.

ACKNOWLEDGEMENTS

Grateful thanks are extended to the following contributors of photographs not only for their use in this book but for their kind patience and long term loan of negatives/photographs whilst this book was being compiled.

D. ALEXANDER MORECAMBE	G. D. APPLEYARD MIDDLESBROUGH	P. BARBER TAMWORTH
H. H. BLEADS BIRMINGHAM	R. S. CARPENTER BIRMINGHAM	A. DART HOVE
C. FIFIELD LONDON	P. GARDNER NORBURY	J. D. GOMERSALL SHEFFIELD
R. GRACE BASINGSTOKE	S. GRADIDGE CHALFONT ST. GILES	D. HARRISON CHAPELTOWN
R. W. HINTON GLOUCESTER	C. HUGHES AMESBURY	A. C. INGRAM WISBECH
G. JINKS BIRMINGHAM	D. K. JONES MOUNTAIN ASH	B. J. MILLER BARRY
D. OAKES HITCHIN	R. PICTON WOLVERHAMPTON	W. G. PIGGOTT HADDENHAM
N. E. PREEDY HUCCLECOTE	B. RANDS WESTON-SUPER-MARE	K. L. SEAL ANDOVERSFORD
G. W. SHARPE BARNSLEY	K. SHIPLEY OSSETT	C. P. STACEY STONY STRATFORD
M. S. STOKES MARPLE	D. TITHERIDGE FAREHAM	S. TURNBULL MILTON OF CAMPSIE
R. TURNER SHEFFIELD	A. WAKEFIELD DRONFIELD	T. WARD NORTHAMPTON
T. WRIGHT SLOUGH		

Further books in this series which are available are as follows:

BRITISH RAILWAYS STEAMING THROUGH THE SIXTIES – Volume One.

BRITISH RAILWAYS STEAMING THROUGH THE SIXTIES – Volume Two.

BRITISH RAILWAYS STEAMING THROUGH THE SIXTIES – Volume Three.

BRITISH RAILWAYS STEAMING ON THE WESTERN REGION – Volume One.

BRITISH RAILWAYS STEAMING ON THE LONDON MIDLAND REGION – Volume One

Other titles available from Defiant Publications.

WHAT HAPPENED TO STEAM – Volumes 1 to 50.

CHASING STEAM ON SHED

BR STEAM SHED ALLOCATIONS – Parts 1 to 3. WR sheds 81A-89C.

Front Cover – BR Class 5 4-6-0 No 73022 speeds through Weybridge on a down ballast train on Sunday 27th March 1966. (W. G. Piggott)

ISBN 0 946857 04 0   (C) P. B. HANDS/C. RICHARDS 1985

INTRODUCTION

BRITISH RAILWAYS STEAMING THROUGH THE SIXTIES – Volume Four is the fourth of a series of books designed to give the ordinary, everyday steam photographic enthusiast of the 1960's a chance to participate in and give pleasure to others whilst recapturing the twilight days of steam.

In this series, wherever possible, no famous names will be found, but the content and quality of the majority of photographs will be second to none. The photographs chosen have been carefully selected to give a mixture of action and shed scenes from many parts of British Railways, whilst utilising a balanced cross-section of locomotives of GWR, SR, LMS & BR origins.

As steam declined, especially from 1966 onwards, the choice of locomotive classes and locations also dwindled. Rather than include the nowadays more traditional preserved locomotive photographs in the latter days of steam, the reader will find more locomotives of SR, LMS & BR backgrounds included towards the end of the book.

The majority of the photographs used in Volume Four have been contributed by readers from Peter Hands series of booklets entitled "What Happened to Steam" and from readers of Volumes One to Three of "BR Steaming Through the Sixties". In normal circumstances these may have been hidden from the public eye for ever.

The continuation of this series and individual regional albums depends upon you the reader. If you feel you have suitable photographic material of BR steam locomotives from 1950-1968 and wish to contribute them towards this series and other future publications please contact either:

<table>
<tr><td>Peter Hands,
190 Yoxall Road,
Shirley, Solihull,
West Midlands B90 3RN.</td><td>OR</td><td>Colin Richards,
28 Kendrick Close,
Damson Parkway, Solihull,
West Midlands B92 0QD.</td></tr>
</table>

CONTENTS

1) GWR *Modified Hall* Class 4-6-0 No 6972
Beningbrough Hall. (S. Gradidge).

2) SR Unrebuilt *Battle of Britain* Class 4-6-2 No
34076 *41 Squadron.* (S. Gradidge).

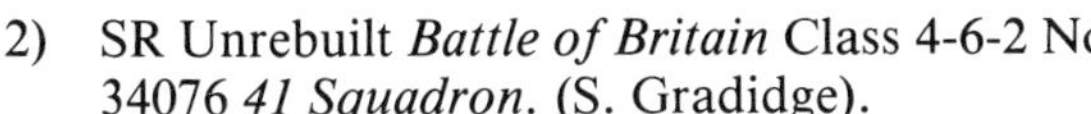

3) LMS *Royal Scot* Class 4-6-0- No 46118 *Royal
Welch Fusilier.* (S. Gradidge).

4) LNER A1 Class 4-6-2 No 60125 *Scottish
Union.* (R. Picton).

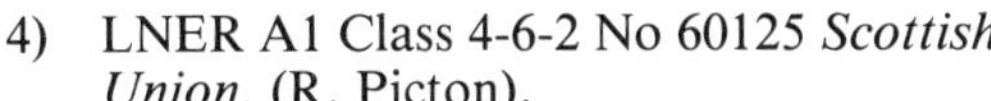

5) BR Class 5 4-6-0 No 73082 *Camelot.*
(S. Gradidge).

CHAPTER ONE – 1960

6) SR N Class 2-6-0 No 31868 with safety valves lifting awaits departure from East Grinstead in July 1960 with a local passenger train. 31868 was based at 75B Redhill which survived as a steam depot until September 1965. (Christopher Fifield)

7) GWR 1400 Class 0-4-2T No 1451 in immaculate condition is the centre-piece of a delightful scene of rural tranquility on 17th June 1960. Photographed at Bampton which was between Tiverton and Dulverton. (N. E. Preedy)

8) Robinson Ex. Great Central Class 04 2-8-0 No 63631 from Gorton depot simmers gently outside 27F Brunswick (Liverpool) shed on 23rd October 1960. This former Cheshire Lines Railway shed was situated in cramped conditions and was closed completely in September 1961. (P. Gardner)

9) LMS *Jubilee* Class 4-6-0- No 45569 *Tasmania* is a visitor to 84G Shrewsbury in March 1960. Based at 55A Leeds (Holbeck) *Tasmania* impatiently blows off steam as if annoyed by the *not to be moved* notice attached to the front buffer beam. (G. W. Sharpe)

10) BR Class 4 2-6-4T No 80038 from 73F Ashford in begrimed condition is in company with two SR Q1 Class 0-6-0's in equally filthy external appearance in the yard at St. Leonards shed on 2nd September 1960. This depot closed as a main shed in September 1958 but continued to service locomotives for some considerable time after. (R. Picton)

11) The driver of LNER Class A2 4-6-2 No 60520 *Owen Tudor* appears to be deep in thought as he waits for the *right away* from Grantham in August 1960 with a Kings Cross – Newcastle express. (H. H. Bleads)

12) SR Rebuilt *West Country* Class 4-6-2 No 34047 *Callington* in ex. works condition presents a fine picture at the head of an Ilfracombe via Exeter express at Waterloo in April 1960. Waterloo was to be the last London terminus to play host to steam locomotives bidding farewell to them in July 1967. (H. H. Bleads)

13) LMS Class 4F 0-6-0 No 44203 trundles through Kings Heath towards Kings Norton on the Birmingham (New Street) avoiding line with a long rake of mineral wagons in July 1960. These locomotives were a common sight in and around the Birmingham area until 1964/65. (H. H. Bleads)

14) GWR 4300 Class 2-6-0 No 6378 from 89C Machynlleth shed at rest in the yard at 84G Shrewsbury in July 1960. Many of these handsome and versatile locomotives were employed on the ex. Cambrian lines to the west of Shrewsbury and were often seen in tandem on heavy holiday expresses during the summer months. (G. W. Sharpe)

15) LNER Q6 Class 0-8-0 No 63451 from 51L Thornaby is noted dead in the shed yard at 51A Darlington on 11th June 1960 in company with several other ex. LNER types including a V2 Class 2-6-2, a K1 Class 2-6-0 and a J27 Class 0-6-0. (M. S. Stokes)

16) BR Class 2 2-6-2T No 84001 drifts into Bangor station with a local stopping train in June 1960. These ungainly looking locomotives introduced in 1953 were not very popular and all were withdrawn from service by the end of 1965. (R. W. Hinton)

17) SR Class 02 0-4-4T No 20 *Shanklin* climbs away from Ryde on the Isle of Wight in August 1960 with a local passenger. These ageing locomotives and equally ancient coaching stock survived in regular service until the end of 1966. (N. E. Preedy)

18) LNER Class A3 4-6-2 No 60055 *Woolwinder* at Kings Cross station in March 1960 after arriving with an express from Leeds. *Woolwinder* is waiting for the empty stock to be removed before making its way to 34A Kings Cross shed. Fitted with double chimney and small smoke deflectors *Woolwinder* was to be withdrawn the following year. (H. H. Bleads)

19) A fine view from the platform of Worcester Shrub station into the shed yard at 85A Worcester in August 1960. On show are a selection of ex. GWR tank engines and 4-6-0's along with an ex. LMS Class 8F 2-8-0. Worcester shed remained open to steam until the end of 1965. (H. H. Bleads)

20) LMS Class 4 2-6-4T (Fowler) No 42324 resides in the shed yard at 56F Low Moor in July 1960. Low Moor was one of the last depots on the North Eastern Region to remain open to steam finally closing its doors in October 1967. (G. W. Sharpe)

21) GWR *Castle* Class 4-6-0 No 7025 *Sudeley Castle* based at Shrewsbury shed arrives at Exeter (St. Davids) station with the 5.30pm express to Plymouth in September 1960. *Sudeley Castle* was to gain fame by taking part in the Ian Allan railtour on 9th May 1964 on the Taunton-Plymouth section covering the almost 83 miles in 98 minutes. (R. Picton)

22) SR Unrebuilt *Battle of Britain* Class 4-6-2 No 34055 *Fighter Pilot* in pristine condition is a visitor from 75A Brighton to 71B Bournemouth in August 1960. *Fighter Pilot* was one of the first members of the class to be withdrawn from service in June 1963. (G. W. Sharpe)

23) The crew of LMS Class 3F 0-6-0T No 47422 take a break from ballast train duties at Ashchurch on a July Sunday in 1960. The train is working 'wrong line'. As can be seen by the wooden station board Ashchurch was once the junction for Tewkesbury, Evesham, Alcester and Redditch. (H. H. Bleads)

24) BR Class 9F 2-10-0 No 92030 simmers gently in the shed yard at 16D Annesley on 20th July 1960. This former Great Central Railway shed had many of these fine locomotives based here for working the high speed coal trains over the ex. GC system. In the left background is one of the Annesley based Robinson 2-8-0's No. 63591. (C. Richards)

25) LMS Jubilee Class 4-6-0 No 45722 *Defence* shares the shed yard with a Class 8F 2-8-0 at 2B Nuneaton in May 1961. Observe the fine signal gantry in the background. Nuneaton shed continued to play host to steam until June 1966. (C. Hughes)

26)   Scene at Kingswear terminus on 10th April 1961 showing GWR 5700 Class 0-6-0PT No 3796 shunting, *Warship* Class Diesel No D826 *Jupiter* on the *Torbay Express* and on the turntable is GWR *Castle* Class 4-6-0 No 5024 *Carew Castle*. To the left of the picture is a paddle steamer which used to operate between Dartmouth and Totnes. (H. H. Bleads)

27)   LNER Class B1 4-6-0 No 61010 *Wildebeeste* from 50B Hull (Dairycoates) is well away from its home territory as it simmers gently outside 21A Saltley shed on 19th March 1961. This large Birmingham depot closed to steam in March 1967. (P. Gardner)

28)   With its safety valves lifting and sporting a variety of discs and train reporting numbers SR Rebuilt *Merchant Navy* Class 4-6-2 No 35021 *New Zealand Line* awaits departure from Waterloo with the down *Royal Wessex* to Weymouth on 15th July 1961. (G. W. Sharpe)

29)   LMS *Coronation* Class 4-6-2 No 46247 *City of Liverpool* takes on refreshment whilst pausing at Hellifield with an RCTS special from Leeds on 9th July 1961. The leading and centre coaches are of Gresley vintage. (G. W. Sharpe)

30) The evening sunlight enhances the fine lines of BR Class 9F 2-10-0 No 92228 at rest in the shed yard at 81F Oxford in February 1961. Constructed in July 1958 and fitted with a double chimney 92228 had a life span of less than nine years. (G. W. Sharpe)

31) GWR 5600 Class 0-6-2T No 5613 takes shelter under the steel corrugated awning at Ferndale depot on 11th March 1961. This depot of Taff Vale Railway origin was a sub shed of 88F Treherbert and survived until September 1964. (D. K. Jones)

32) Scene at 21E Monument Lane (Birmingham) shed in April 1961. In the foreground there is a line-up of stored locomotives comprising of a variety of LMS types – 0-6-0's & 4-4-0's Nos. 44506, 40678 (left) & 40936, 41168, 40692 (right). Monument Lane closed in February 1962. (H. H. Bleads)

33) WD Class 8F 2-8-0 No 90676 heads a train of pipe-laden bogie wagons towards the southern portal of Bodenham tunnel on the Hereford-Shrewsbury line in May 1961. (H. H. Bleads)

34) Kings Cross based LNER Class A4 4-6-2 No 60026 *Miles Beevor* passes Low Moor with a Bradford express in May 1961. *Miles Beevor* was transferred to the Scottish Region in October 1963 and survived in service until December 1965. Stored at a variety of locations it was not scrapped until January 1968. (G. W. Sharpe)

35) SR E2 Class 0-6-0T No 32102 and *King Arthur* Class 4-6-0 No 30453 *King Arthur* look in good external condition despite being in store and waiting to be scrapped at Eastleigh Works in October 1961. (T. Wright)

36)   GWR *King* Class 4-6-0 No 6004 *King George III* is fresh from overhaul on 30th July 1961 and waits to be reunited with its tender at Swindon Works. Based at 88A Cardiff (Canton) *King George III* was withdrawn from service twelve months later and after a period of storage made its own way to Swindon for cutting up. (R. Picton)

37)   LMS Class 2P 4-4-0 No 40696 stands in an isolated position at the rear of 82F Bath Green Park shed on 15th January 1961. Despite the sacked chimney and stored appearance this locomotive survived in service until July 1962. For many years 40696 and its sister engines along with the S & D 2-8-0's were the mainstay of many services over the Somerset & Dorset. (P. Gardner)

38) SR *Schools* Class 4-4-0 No 30912 *Downside* drifts into Basingstoke station with a semi-fast train on 13th May 1961. In 1957 all forty members of the class were at depots on the Central and Eastern divisions but due to electrification many examples were transferred to the Western division. By the end of 1962 this splendid class of 4-4-0's was rendered extinct. (R. Picton)

39) LNER Class A1 4-6-2 No 60140 *Balmoral* accelerates past the camera with the 13.00 hrs express from Stockton-on-Tees and heads south for its ultimate destination of Colchester – October 1961. (G. D. Appleyard)

40) GWR 1500 Class 0-6-0PT No 1508 and 5600 Class 0-6-2T No 5612 (87F Llanelly) stand bunker to bunker in the shed yard at 88A Cardiff (Canton) on 20th August 1961. Canton was an extremely busy steam shed with a variety of passenger and freight locomotives based there. It was however closed to steam in September 1962 most of its surviving stock being transferred to the reopened Cardiff East Dock shed. (R. Picton)

41) Ex. Caledonian Railway Class 2P 0-4-4T No 55203 on station pilot duties at Glasgow (St. Enoch) on 19th June 1961. 55203 was withdrawn in December of the same year and during 1966 St. Enoch station closed completely. (G. W. Sharpe)

42)	BR *Britannia* Class 4-6-2 No 70009 *Alfred the Great* in filthy condition passes Ely North Junction with an express to Cambridge on 5th August 1961. Based at Norwich shed for a number of years *Alfred the Great* was transferred to March shed approximately one month after this picture was taken. (G. W. Sharpe)

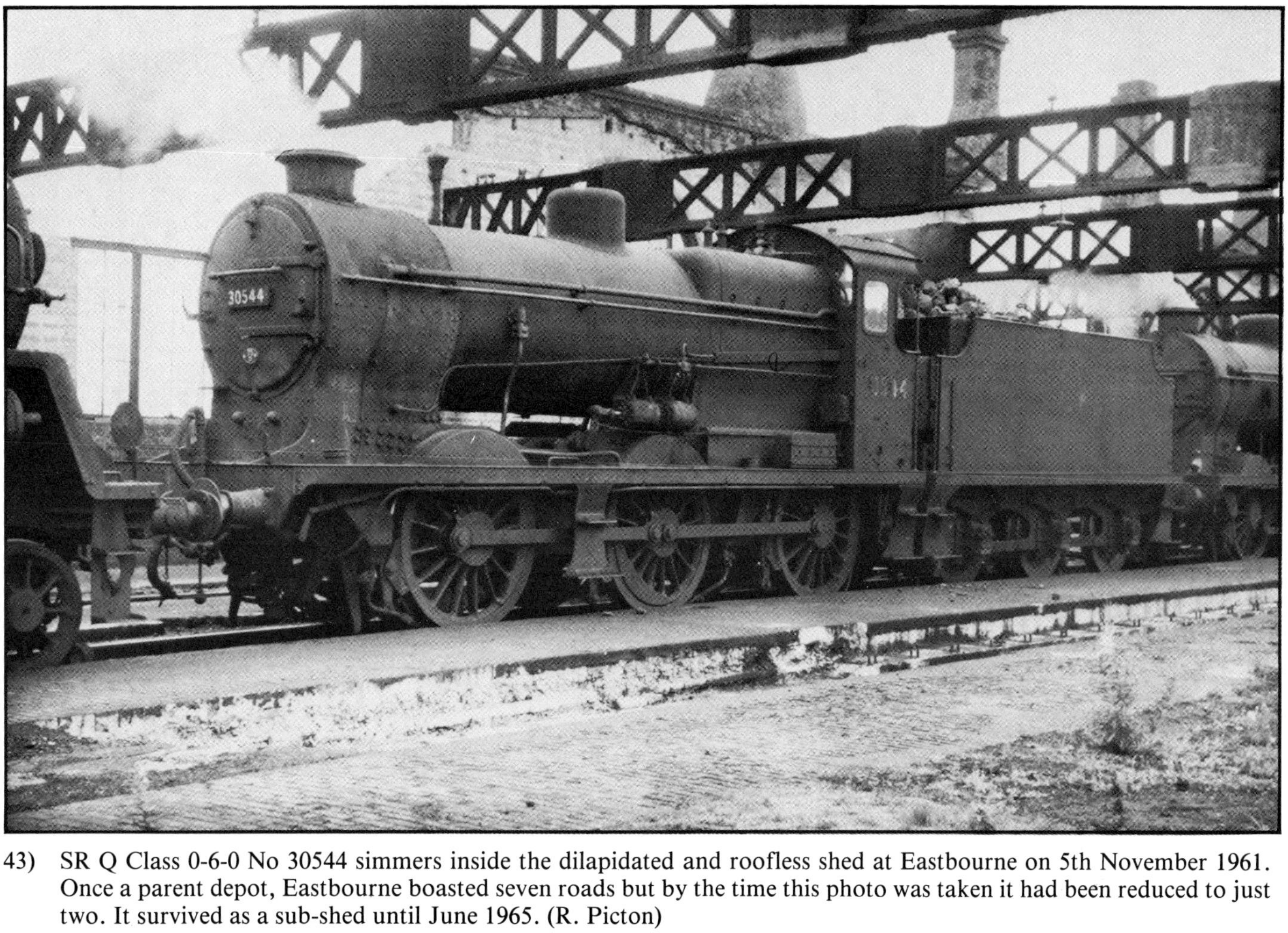

43)	SR Q Class 0-6-0 No 30544 simmers inside the dilapidated and roofless shed at Eastbourne on 5th November 1961. Once a parent depot, Eastbourne boasted seven roads but by the time this photo was taken it had been reduced to just two. It survived as a sub-shed until June 1965. (R. Picton)

44)   GWR *King* Class 4-6-0 No 6002 *King William IV* is held partly aloft by a massive chain inside 84A Wolverhampton (Stafford Road) on 5th August 1962. A month later this engine was on show to the public at Birmingham (Snow Hill) prior to the Birkenhead – Paddington expresses being taken over by diesel power. (R. Picton)

45)   The annual RCTS *EAST MIDLANDER* railtours from Nottingham were well known for producing odd pairings of locomotives over foreign lines. In this view SR *Schools* Class 4-4-0 No 30925 *Cheltenham* and MR 2P 4-4-0 No 40646 are seen taking water at Church Fenton. On this tour Darlington Works and shed were the venue on 13th May 1962. (N. E. Preedy)

46)   LNER Class B1 4-6-0 No 61087 from Doncaster shed is a stranger in the camp, at rest in the shed yard at 85C Gloucester (Barnwood) on a bleak winters day on 13th January 1962. This type of locomotive was a fairly common sight during the summer months but during the winter was a comparative rarity. (C. Richards)

47) The hiss of escaping steam from the safety valves of S & D Class 7F 2-8-0 No 53809 coupled with BR Class 5 4-6-0 No 73049 disturbs the peace and quiet of the countryside around Midford as they arrive with a Birmingham-Bournemouth express on 1st September 1962. (N. E. Preedy)

48) The late evening sunshine heralds the arrival of LNER A3 Class 4-6-2 No 60060 *The Tetrarch* as it sweeps its Newcastle-Kings Cross express around the curve to the north of York station on 21st July 1962. The lines to the right of the picture go towards Scarborough. (D. Alexander)

49) GWR 6400 Class 0-6-0PT No 6408 in the shed yard at 82B St. Philips Marsh on 28th July 1962. Withdrawn from service from 88H Tondu in February 1962 it may have possibly been used as a stationary boiler for a while (observe the cut down chimney) and was presumably at St. Philips Marsh whilst in transit to Swindon Works for scrapping. (R. Picton)

50) SR Rebuilt *Merchant Navy* Class 4-6-2 No 35014 *Nederland Line* in ex. works condition shows off its handsome profile whilst in the shed yard at 71A Eastleigh on 15th April 1962. (R. Picton)

51)   LMS Class 4 2-6-4T (Fowler) No 42317 in fine external condition poses for the camera in the shed yard at 55G Huddersfield in company with an unidentified WD Class 8F 2-8-0 in April 1962. Huddersfield shed also known as Hillhouse closed to steam on January 1967 and completely in November 1967. (G. W. Sharpe)

52)   Saltley based BR Class 9F 2-10-0 No 92129 casts a giant shadow over the Worcestershire countryside as it maintains masterly control over its heavy train on the severe down-grade of the Lickey incline between Blackwell and Bromsgrove on 25th August 1962. (R. Picton)

53) A typical scene at Oxford during the days of steam taken on 30th June 1962. On the left is GWR *Grange* Class 4-6-0 No 6803 *Bucklebury Grange* on the 1.11pm express to Birkenhead. In the centre GWR 6100 Class 2-6-2T No 6154 arrives with the 1.20pm local to Princes Risborough and on the right are a group of trainspotters. (R. Picton)

54) SR Q1 Class 0-6-0 No 33039 from 70B Feltham is noted dead in the shed yard at 71A Eastleigh on 15th April 1962. Note the old style BR ensignia on the tender. (R. Picton)

55)   The elderly but well proportioned lines of LNW Class 7F 0-8-0 No 49381 are lit up by a weak sunshine in the shed yard
at 8F Springs Branch Wigan on 31st March 1962. This depot in use mainly as a freight shed remained open to steam
until the end of 1967. (R. Picton)

56)   BR *Clan* Class 4-6-2 No 72005 *Clan Macgregor* from Carlisle (Kingmoor) shed is a visitor to 67F Stranraer on 23rd
June 1962. By the look of the express headlamps *Clan Macgregor* is about ready to take charge of an express to
Carlisle. Note the damaged running plate. (D. Harrison)

57)   SR 02 Class 0-4-4T No 16 *Ventnor* heading a local train to Shanklin awaits the arrival of sister locomotive No 17 *Seaview* on the 5.10pm local from Shanklin-Ryde. Photographed at Sandown, Isle of Wight on 14th July 1962. (R. Picton)

58)   LNER A4 Class 4-6-2 No 60034 *Lord Faringdon* takes on water at Retford in June 1962. Photographed on a loose coupled freight *Lord Faringdon* presumably was on a running in turn after overhaul at Doncaster Works. This locomotive was transferred to the Scottish Region in October 1963 and survived until August 1966. (G. W. Sharpe)

59) BR Class 4 2-6-0 No 76015 pilots SR Unrebuilt *West Country* 4-6-2 No 34043 *Coombe Martin* into Midford Station on 1st September 1962 with a Bournemouth-Bradford express which is made up predominantly of Gresley stock. (N. E. Preedy)

60) G.C. Class 01 2-8-0 No 63795 simmers gently in the yard adjacent to the shed building at 41H Staveley G.C. on 3.4.62. This locomotive was based at Staveley G.C. from 12.59 until withdrawn in 10.63 and was scrapped at Doncaster Works in 2.64. The shed closed completely on 14.6.65. (R. Picton)

61)   LNW Class 7F 0-8-0 No 48930 at rest in the sidings at Walsall in October 1962. Like 48930 a large number of these locomotives were allocated to Bescot shed and two of their kind Nos. 48895 and 49361 survived in service until December 1964. (R. S. Carpenter)

62)   A few wisps of escaping steam is all that signifies that GWR *Castle* Class 4-6-0 No 7009 *Athelney Castle* is alive and well. Photographed on 4th August 1962 outside 85A Worcester *Athelney Castle* is already prepared for the up *Cathedrals Express* to Paddington. (R. Picton)

63) This close-up of the front end of LNER A2 Class 4-6-2 No 60532 *Blue Peter* clearly shows the handsome profile of this modern pacific. Photographed at 62B Dundee Tay Bridge shed on 2nd August 1963 *Blue Peter* was a regular standby locomotive for a number of years along with sister engines 60528 *Tudor Minstrel* and 60530 *Sayajirao*. *Blue Peter* is preserved at Dinting. (B. J. Miller)

64) LMS *Royal Scot* Class 4-6-0 No 46130 *The West Yorkshire Regiment* presents a sad sight minus nameplates and with a sacked chimney stored in a siding at 55C Farnley Junction on 28th July 1963. For a number of years this engine along with sister locomotives Nos. 46103/8/9/12/13/17/33/45 was based at 55A Leeds (Holbeck) before being ousted by diesels. (G. W. Sharpe)

65) Immingham based BR *Britannia* Class 4-6-2 No 70037 *Hereward the Wake* nears West Leake on the ex. Great Central main line south of Nottingham with a Grimsby-Whitland Class C fish train on 30th May 1963. (K. L. Seal)

66) GWR *Manor* Class 4-6-0 No 7810 *Draycott Manor* departs from platform four of Shrewsbury station with the down *Cambrian Coast Express* on 2nd August 1963. These popular locomotives were in constant use over the old Cambrian system up to the end of 1965. (K. L. Seal)

67) SR Unrebuilt *West Country* Class 4-6-2 No 34094 *Mortehoe* in immaculate external condition arrives at Fleet with an express to Waterloo on 3rd June 1963. Of the 110 members of the W.C. & B.B. class, sixty six were *West Country* of which twenty three remained in unrebuilt form. (D. Oakes)

68) LNER Class J38 0-6-0 No 65934 is veiled in smoke and steam outside 64A St. Margarets shed on 3rd August 1963. All thirty five members of the class were based in Scotland and spent most of their lives hauling coal trains. 65934 was the last of the class and was allocated to 62C Dunfermline when this photograph was taken. (B. J. Miller)

69) BR Class 9F 2-10-0 No 92214 is ex. works and minus its tender in the yard at Crewe Works in May 1963. 92214 entered service during October 1959 at 84C Banbury, moved on to 86A Newport (Ebbw Junction) in November 1961 and finally to 86E Severn Tunnel Junction during July 1964 before being withdrawn in August 1965. (R. Turner)

70)   Saltley based LMS Class 5 4-6-0 No 44663 makes a fine shot as it speeds through Mangotsfield station on the outskirts of Bristol with a fitted freight in November 1963. (G. W. Sharpe)

71)   The pioneer GWR 4700 Class 2-8-0 No 4700 minus safety valve cover rots away in a siding at 81A Old Oak Common on 19th October 1963. Withdrawn from service in October 1962 4700 spent some eighteen months in store at Old Oak Common and Southall before being scrapped by Kings of Norwich in March 1964. (G. W. Sharpe)

72) LMS Class 4F 0-6-0 No 44060, LMS *Coronation* Class 4-6-2 No 46255 *City of Hereford* and LMS Class 5 4-6-0 No 44991 (66B Motherwell) are photographed outside the southern end of 12A Carlisle (Kingmoor) on 16th June 1963. Kingmoor remained open to steam until the end of 1967 being replaced by a diesel depot on the other side of the main lines. (N. E. Preedy)

73) SR Unrebuilt *Battle of Britain* Class 4-6-2 No 34057 *Biggin Hill* its paintwork gleaming drifts through Millbrook with an express in the summer of 1963. *Biggin Hill* was one of forty-four *Battle of Britain* engines of which twenty-seven were unrebuilt. (G. W. Sharpe)

74) 34E New England shed on a misty 1st September 1963. On view are two BR Class 9F 2-10-0's one of which is No 92142, an unidentified LNER B1 Class 4-6-0 and LNER A4 Class 4-6-2 No 60010 *Dominion of Canada*. After the closure of 34A Kings Cross in June 1963 the surviving A4's were transferred here. Of their numbers 60006/7/10/26/34 were transferred to Scotland in October 1963. *Dominion of Canada* is preserved in Montreal. (K. L. Seal)

75) WD Class 8F No 90384 in reasonable condition stands in the shed yard at 41F Mexborough on 9th November 1963. This once busy ex. Great Central Railway depot closed completely in March 1964. (G. W. Sharpe)

76) A grubby GWR *Castle* Class 4-6-0 No 5085 *Evesham Abbey* minus its front numberplate departs from Bristol (Temple Meads) with the 1.50pm express to Weston-super-Mare on 31st August 1963. Allocated to 82B St. Philips Marsh *Evesham Abbey* was withdrawn from service in February of the following year. (R. Picton)

77) SR Unrebuilt *West Country* Class 4-6-2 No 34019 *Bideford* stands outside Brighton station in May 1963. *Bideford* was one of a batch of light pacifics allocated to 75A Brighton but due to electrification and other modernisation all were transferred away by September 1963. (G. W. Sharpe)

78) LNER A3 Class 4-6-2 No 60106 *Flying Fox* approaches Egmanton Crossing on the East Coast Main Line north of Newark with the 08.35 hrs *Bergen Line* boat train from Newcastle Tyne Commission Quay-Kings Cross on 1st June 1963. (K. L. Seal)

79) BR Class 9F 2-10-0 No 92121 throws a plume of white smoke into the air as it approaches Hathern on the Midland main line north of Loughborough with a southbound freight on 11th May 1963. (K. L. Seal)

80) GWR 5100 Class 2-6-2T No 4166 in good external condition is noted at rest in the shed yard at 88B Cardiff (Radyr) on 8th March 1963. This depot of GWR origin was a sub shed of Cardiff Cathays until December 1957 when it became a parent depot. It was closed to steam in July 1965. (D. K. Jones)

81) Leeds (Holbeck) based LMS *Jubilee* Class 4-6-0 No 45573 *Newfoundland* enters Trent station on the Midland main line with a Bradford-St. Pancras special on 15th April 1963. (K. L. Seal)

CHAPTER FIVE—1964

82) A footplate view from the cab of SR Unrebuilt *Battle of Britain* Class 4-6-2 No 34079 *141 Squadron* as it approaches Winchfield with a Clapham Junction-West of England milk train on 19th August 1964. Judging by the state of the air smoothed casing *141 Squadron* is in need of overhaul. (R. Grace)

83)   LMS *Coronation* Class 4-6-2 No 46245 *City of London* is on parade at the Derby Works open day on 29th August 1964. Despite its smart appearance *City of London* was withdrawn just over one month later along with the remaining survivors thus rendering this fine class of locomotives extinct. (P. Barber)

84)   GWR 6100 Class 2-6-2T No 6144 brings the stock of a local passenger train into Pontypool Road station on 29th February 1964. Little remains today of this once busy station which boasted a large allocation of locomotives at its own depot which closed in May 1965. (R. Picton)

85)   LMS Class 2 2-6-0 No 46520 stands at Pwllheli with the 10.25am local passenger train to Dovey Junction on 13th July 1964. Many examples of this class had a long association with the railways in this region. (R. Picton)

86)   Honiton station can hardly be classed as packed with potential customers as BR Class 5 4-6-0 No 73161 arrives with a passenger train on 18th May 1964. (R. Picton)

87) GWR *Castle* Class 4-6-0 No 7019 *Fowey Castle* in deplorable external condition prepares for the road at 2D Banbury shed on 15th November 1964. Based at 2B Oxley *Fowey Castle* was one of only thirteen surviving members of this once proud class, the others being Nos. 5014/26/42/56/63/89, 7012/22/23/24/29/34. (Terry Ward)

88) All the power and grace of the magnificent LNER A4 Class 4-6-2's is shown up in this photograph of 60009 *Union of South Africa* as it stands in the shed yard at 65B St. Rollox on a winters day in 1964. *Union of South Africa* which was based at Ferryhill (Aberdeen) survived in service until June 1966 and is privately preserved. (G. W. Sharpe)

89)   Begrimed SR Rebuilt *Merchant Navy* Class 4-6-2 No 35027 *Port Line* is photographed at Waterloo on 6th August 1964 with a down express to Bournemouth. *Port Line* is now preserved at the Swindon & Cricklade Railway. The fellow photographer is equipped with the *standard* trainspotters duffle bag. (G. W. Sharpe)

90)   LMS Class 3F 0-6-0T No 47623 latterly of 82F Bath Green Park lies condemned and unwanted in the sidings at Swindon Works on 26th April 1964 prior to scrapping. Only a handful of these locomotives saw service on the Western Region mostly around the Bath, Bristol, Bromsgrove and Gloucester areas. (R. Picton)

91)   The oil-can is applied to ex. GC 04 Class 2-8-0 No 63628 before it leaves the shed yard at 50A York with a freight for
its home base of Frodingham, Scunthorpe on 1st September 1964. This type of locomotive was a common sight at
York until 1965. (M. S. Stokes)

92)   During the latter years of steam many fine engines succumbed to a life of grime. GWR *Hall* Class 4-6-0 No 6908
Downham Hall from 82E Bristol Barrow Road is no exception. Shorn of nameplates and front number *Downham
Hall* is at Oxford with an excursion in September 1964 being *admired* by a group of spotters on the opposite platform.
(D. K. Jones)

93)   In the 1960's railtours started in earnest. BR *Britannia* Class 4-6-2 No 70020 *Mercury* from 1A Willesden enters the roundhouse at 50A York after arriving at York with the *Home Counties Railway* Society special on 4th October 1964. (B. J. Miller)

94)   GWR 2251 Class 0-6-0 No 2242 is photographed in the shed yard at 86C Hereford in August 1964. 2242 was transferred to Gloucester in November 1964 and was withdrawn in May 1965. Hereford shed closed late in 1964. (G. W. Sharpe)

95) SR N Class 2-6-0 No 31408 from 70C Guildford stands in Nine Elms goods yard with a breakdown train in May 1964. (A. C. Ingram)

96) Sunlight and shadow at Huddersfield station as LMS Class 5 4-6-0 No 45347 from Fleetwood shed prepares to leave the station with a local passenger train in September 1964. (B. J. Miller)

97) SR Unrebuilt *Battle of Britain* Class 4-6-2 No 34065 *Hurricane* reaches the end of the road in a store line at 70D Eastleigh after condemnation. Photographed on 22nd April 1964 *Hurricane* remained in store at Eastleigh before being sent to South Wales for scrapping in November 1964. (D. K. Jones)

98) An immaculate LNER A2 Class 4-6-2 No 60530 *Sayajirao* its tender filled to capacity is photographed in steam in the yard at 62B Dundee Tay Bridge in December 1964. Dundee shed remained open to steam until May 1967. (G. W. Sharpe)

99) In marked contrast to 34065 on the opposite page SR Rebuilt *Battle of Britain* Class 4-6-2 No 34050 *Royal Observer Corps* is photographed in immaculate condition on the turntable at 70A Nine Elms on 1st July 1964. Note the R.O.C. ribbon on the cabside. (N. E. Preedy)

100) After what appears to be a change of engine crews BR *Britannia* Class 4-6-2 No 70007 *Coeur-de-Lion* moves out of Perth station on 1st September 1964 on a somewhat menial duty. The Dundee line is to the right of the picture. (D. K. Jones)

101) WD Class 8F 2-8-0 No 90677 from Hull (Dairycoates) stands in the shed yard at 55H Leeds (Neville Hill) on 2nd September 1965. 733 of these locomotives sometimes known as *bed-irons* were in service on B.R. Leeds (Neville Hill) was one of the last depots on the North Eastern Region to house Pacifics and closed to steam in June 1966. (D. K. Jones)

102) LNER Class A4 4-6-2 No 60019 *Bittern* resides in the repair shop at 65B St. Rollox during 1965. St. Rollox was the depot for the ill fated Glasgow (Buchanan Street) station and closed completely in November 1966. *Bittern* was withdrawn in September 1966 but received a better fate and is preserved at Dinting. (A. C. Ingram)

103) GWR 6100 Class 2-6-2T No 6126 stands in the yard at 81F Oxford on 1st June 1965. This depot was one of the last to play host to steam on the Western Region closing in January 1966. (D. K. Jones)

104)   Bright sunshine outlines the handsome design of this LMS Class 5 4-6-0 No 44889 from Lancaster (Green Ayre) shed
        as it prepares to leave Shipley with an express in July 1965. (G. W. Sharpe)

105)   LNER A2 Class 4-6-2 No 60530 *Sayajirao* in fine fettle prepares to leave Dundee Tay Bridge with the 12.00pm
        express to Glasgow (Buchanan Street) on 4th September 1965. (G. Jinks)

106) BR Class 4 2-6-4T No 80028 from 63A Perth and an unidentified LMS Class 5 4-6-0 stand together in the shed yard at 65B St. Rollox on a sunny day in 1965. (A. C. Ingram)

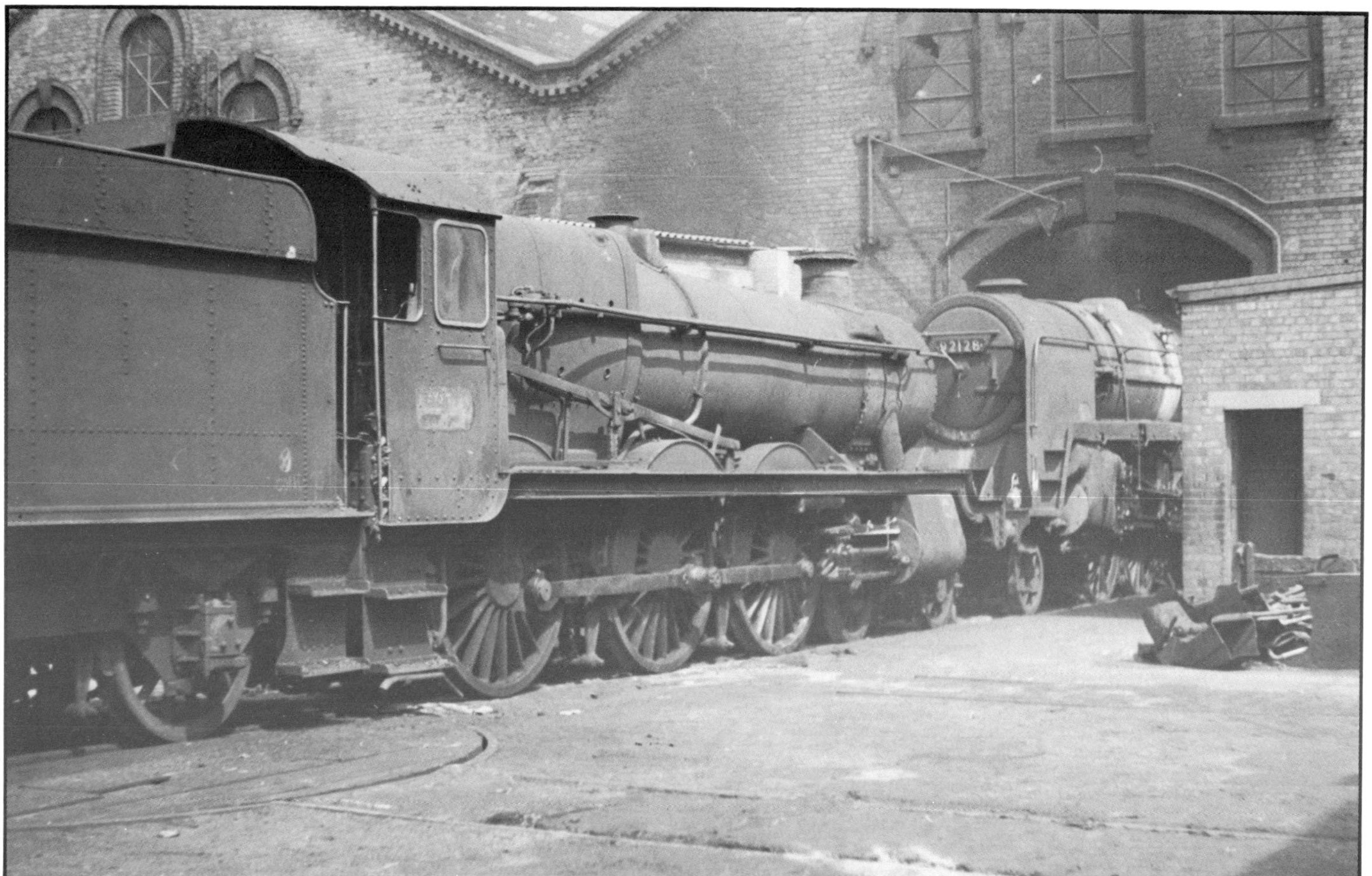

107) GWR *Hall* Class 4-6-0 No 5955 *Garth Hall* condemned and shorn of name and numberplates faces BR Class 9F 2-10-0 No 92128 (2D Banbury) as it peeps out of the shed building at 82E Bristol (Barrow Road) on 13th June 1965. (R. Picton)

108)   LNER A2 Class 4-6-2 No 60512 *Steady Aim* minus coupling rods and nameplates is noted in the yard at 65B St. Rollox around September 1965 and waits for its last journey to the breakers yard. 60512 along with sister engines 60522/24/27/35 were all transferred to 66A Polmadie (Glasgow) in October 1963 but all were withdrawn from service by June 1965. (A. C. Ingram)

109)   In an unkempt condition minus front numberplate, nameplates and safety valve cover GWR *Castle* Class 4-6-0 No 5042 *Winchester Castle* leaves 81C Southall shed and makes for Paddington to head the 4.15pm express to Banbury on 5th April 1965. It comes as no surprise to inform the reader that *Winchester Castle* was withdrawn a few weeks later. (W. G. Piggott)

110)	Two LMS Class 5 4-6-0's one of which is No 44959 lie condemned in the shed yard at 65B St. Rollox around September 1965. Both tenders are devoid of coal. Note the single line tablet catcher apparatus on the cabsides. (A. C. Ingram)

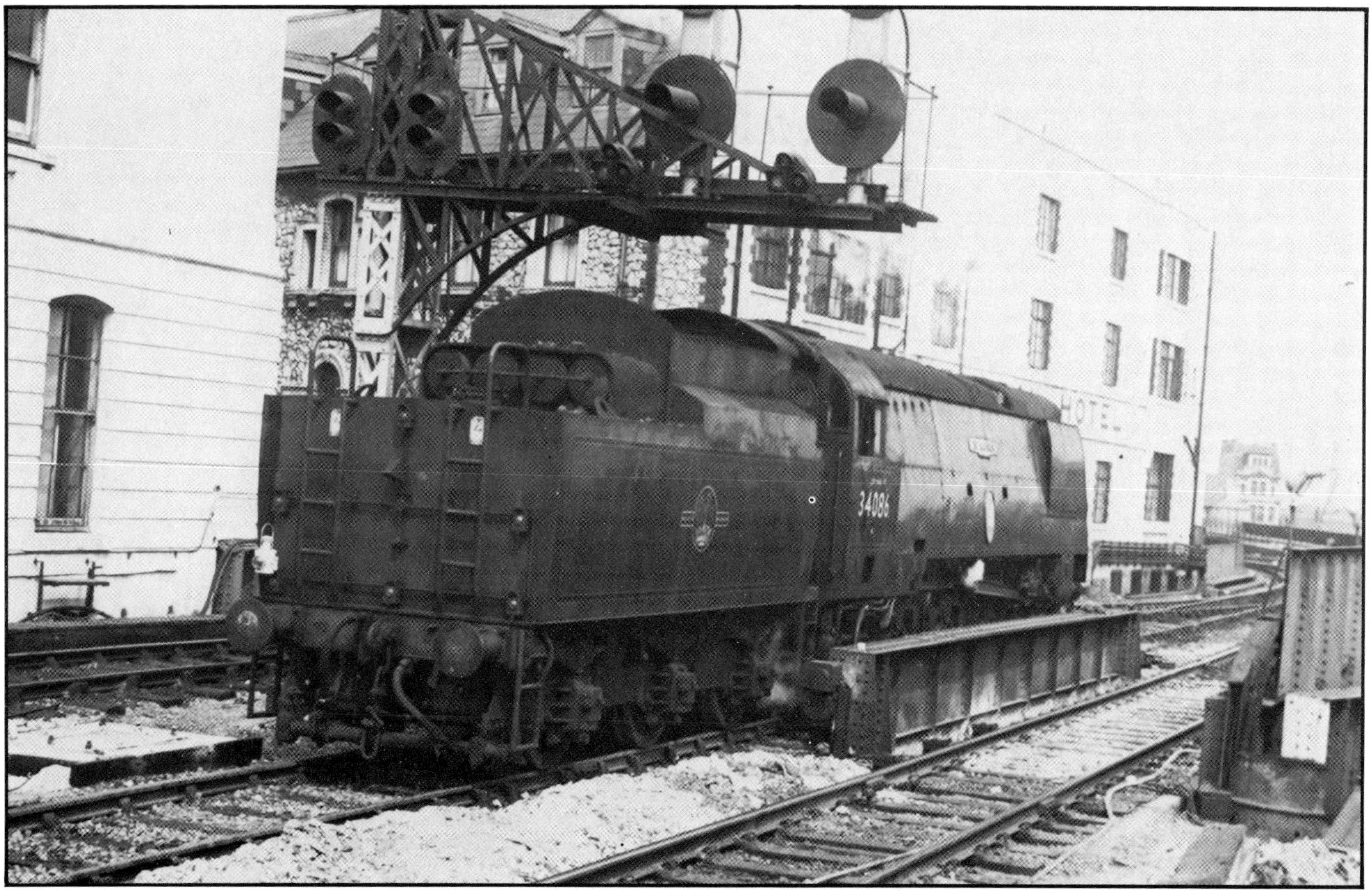

111)	To see a SR locomotive at Cardiff even in busier steam days was the exception to the rule. It was even more remarkable in 1965. SR unrebuilt *Battle of Britain* Class 4-6-2 No. 34086 *219 Squadron* from 70D Eastleigh heads for home light engine on 3rd July 1965 after bringing in the 10.29am express from Portsmouth. (D. K. Jones)

112)   LMS Stanier Class 4 2-6-4 Tanks Nos 42147 and 42285 both condemned are at the side of the shed building at 56F Low Moor on 29th August 1965. A number of these engines were based here and often worked on the Bradford-Leeds section with expresses to and from Kings Cross. (R. Picton)

113)   SR Rebuilt *Battle of Britain* Class 4-6-2 No 34053 *Sir Keith Park* shorn of nameplates and motion waits for its long journey to Barry Docks on 6th December 1965. (D. Titheridge)

114)   Ex. Crosti BR Class 9F 2-10-0 No 92024 from 12A Carlisle (Kingmoor) is the focus of attention despite its quite deplorable condition at the head of a freight train in a goods yard at Bradford in June 1965. (G. W. Sharpe)

115)   LNER B1 Class 4-6-0 No 61308 arrives at Thornton Junction with a lengthy mineral train in October 1965. The nearby Motive Power Depot was a bastion of steam until its closure to steam in November 1966. (G. W. Sharpe)

116) LMS *Jubilee* Class 4-6-0 No 45705 *Seahorse* darkens the sky as it gets to grips with the LCGB *High Peak Railtour* from Cheadle Heath on 18th September 1965. There had been a loco change here with *Flying Scotsman* giving way to *Seahorse*. (N. E. Preedy)

117) GWR 5700 Class 0-6-0PT No 9610 blows off steam in the shed yard of its home depot at 6C Croes Newydd. This former Great Western depot came under London Midland control in 1963 and operated some of the last ex. GWR locomotives late into 1966 and closed to steam in June 1967. Photographed in late 1965. (D. K. Jones)

118)   LMS Class 5 4-6-0 No 44847 passes Wilford near Nottingham with the 07.40hrs Nottingham (Victoria)-Rugby (Central) local passenger train on 12th May 1965. (K. L. Seal)

119)   BR Class 5 4-6-0 No 73114 *Etarre* blows off impatiently as it awaits its next turn of banking duty at Weymouth on 11th September 1965. (R. Picton)

120) The fine profile of this close-up of the front end of SR Unrebuilt *West Country* Class 4-6-2 No 34023 *Blackmore Vale* is clearly shown as the engine simmers gently in the shed yard at 70D Eastleigh on 3rd September 1966. *Blackmore Vale* is preserved on the Bluebell Railway. (D. Titheridge)

121)   LMS Class 5 4-6-0 No 44998 a longstanding occupant of 63A Perth shed stands in bright sunshine in the shed yard on 16th July 1966. 44998 was withdrawn shortly before the depot closed to steam in May 1967. (C. P. Stacey)

122)   Just before the start of a downpour of rain BR Class 5 4-6-0 No 73117 *Vivien* gets under way from Basingstoke with a York-Bournemouth express on 15th October 1966. (N. E. Preedy)

123)   SR Unrebuilt *West Country* Class 4-6-2 No 34006 *Bude* lifts its safety valves standing light engine on a centre road in Eastleigh station on 20th May 1966. (D. Titheridge)

124)   The crew of BR Class 4 2-6-4T No 80011 appear to be having a lecture about the spillage of water from its side tank as it drifts through Swanage on 23rd July 1966. (R. Picton)

125)   LNER Q6 Class 0-8-0 No 63394 prepares to leave 51C West Hartlepool shed on 14th May 1966. This depot with its elderly allocation closed to steam in September 1967. (D. Titheridge)

126)   LMS Class 8F 2-8-0's Nos 48100 and 48364 are bathed in sunlight in the shed yard at 16E Kirkby on 28.2.66. Both of these locomotives were at this time based at Kirkby — No 48100 was transferred to Northwich in April 1966 and No 48364 to Stoke in September 1966. Kirkby shed closed to steam on 3.10.66. (P. Barber)

127)   LMS *Jubilee* Class 4-6-0 No 45581 *Bihar and Orissa* and an unidentified LMS Class 5 4-6-0 pass Farnley Junction with a heavy parcels train in May 1966. (G. W. Sharpe)

128)   SR Rebuilt *West Country* Class 4-6-2 No 34005 *Barnstaple* and BR Class 4 2-6-0 No 76013 both lie condemned in the yard at 70D Eastleigh on 12th October 1966. *Barnstaple* and 76013 were both cut up by Buttigiegs of Newport during 1967. (D. Titheridge)

129) LNER V2 Class 2-6-2 No 60919 is the main line standby locomotive at 62B Dundee Tay Bridge shed on 16th July 1966. Nos. 60831 (50A York) and 60836 (62B Dundee Tay Bridge) were the last representatives of the class being withdrawn in December 1966. (C. P. Stacey)

130) BR Class 5 4-6-0 No 73002 nears Wareham with a four coach semi-fast passenger on 22nd July 1966. From January 1957 73002 served on the London Midland and Eastern Regions before being transferred to the Southern in December 1962. (R. Picton)

131)   LMS Class 5 4-6-0 No 44664 simmers in the shed yard at 9K Bolton on 27th July 1966. Bolton shed was one of the last bastions of steam in the Manchester area, closing down in July 1968. (C. P. Stacey)

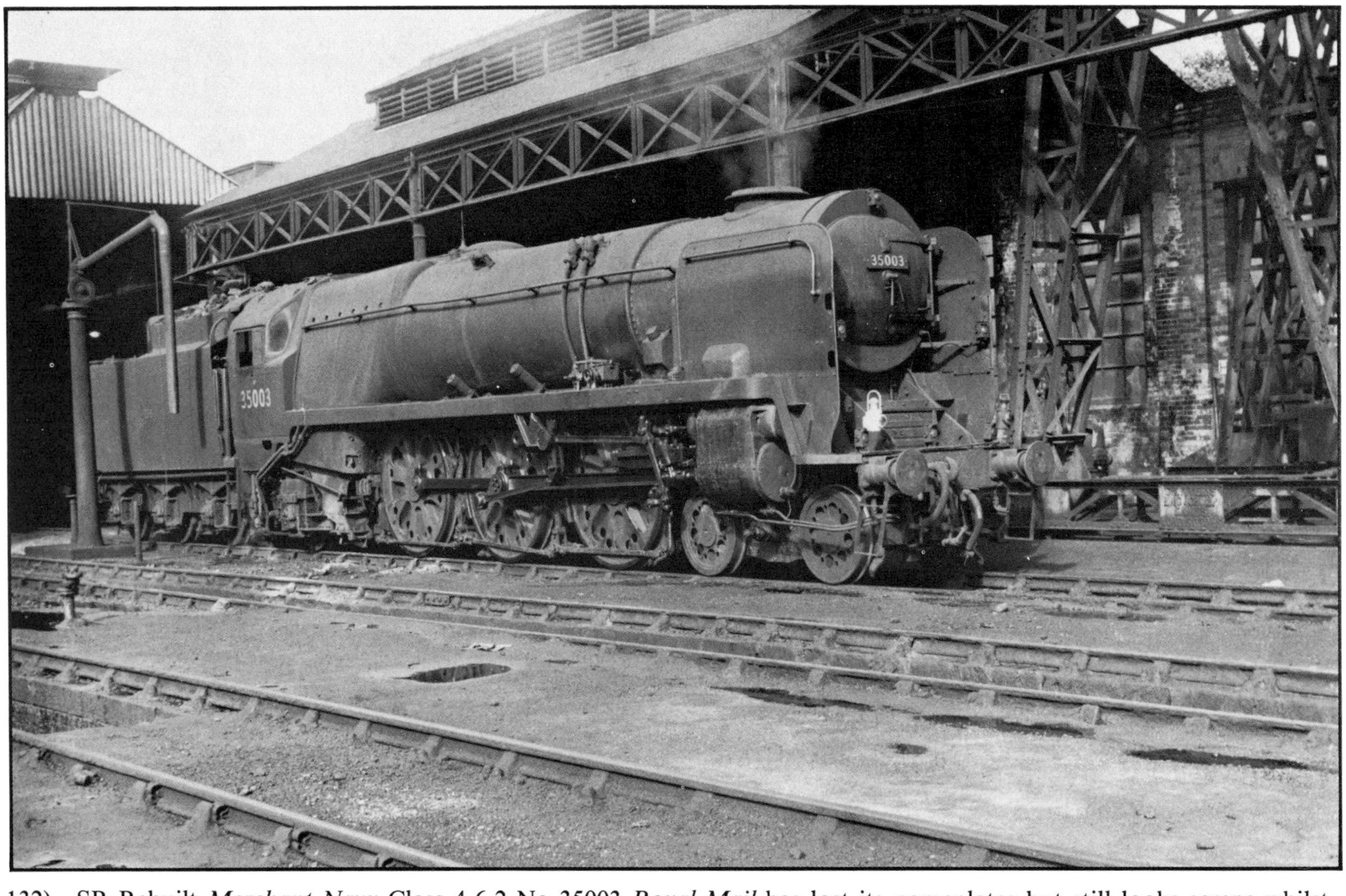

132)   SR Rebuilt *Merchant Navy* Class 4-6-2 No 35003 *Royal Mail* has lost its nameplates but still looks serene whilst waiting its next turn of duty outside the shed building at 70F Bournemouth on 8th October 1966. (D. Titheridge)

133)   BR Class 4 2-6-0 No 76014 nears Wareham with a local passenger train on 22nd July 1966. (R. Picton)

134)   LMS Class 8F 2-8-0 No 48126 from 55B Stourton trundles a mineral train over a viaduct at Catcliffe near Tinsley, Sheffield in March 1966. How modern day coaches have changed since this photograph was taken as the elderly looking example of the day will testify to in the bottom left hand corner. (A. Wakefield)

135)   LMS Class 0F 0-4-0ST No 47001 out of use at 41D Canklow on 2nd May 1966. The number 7001 has been transposed over the BR one. 47001 along with sister engine 47005 survived until December 1966 before the class was rendered extinct. Canklow had closed completely some months before this picture was taken. (R. Picton)

136)   A Southern Pacific wanders far from its home territory on 20th November 1966. SR *Merchant Navy* Class 4-6-2 No 35026 *Lamport & Holt Line* from 70G Weymouth is the subject of youthful admiration at Doncaster whilst hauling the *Williams Deacons Bank Club* special. (B. J. Miller)

137)   A begrimed and stained BR Class 3 2-6-2T No 82018 stands at Waterloo with empty coaching stock on 22nd June
       1966. A number of these locomotives were first transferred to 70A Nine Elms in October 1962 as replacements for the
       more elderly SR tank engines operating from there. (W. G. Piggott)

138)   LMS (Stanier) Class 4 2-6-4T No 42095 rests between banking duties outside 12E Tebay shed on 14th May 1966.
       Tebay shed had a small allocation of these locomotives which were replaced by BR Class 4 4-6-0's in May 1967.
       (C. Richards)

139) LMS Class 5 4-6-0 No 45259 from 12A Carlisle (Kingmoor) is in steam in the shed yard at 55F Bradford (Manningham) in January 1967. Manningham closed around April 1967, 45259 survived a little longer being withdrawn in December of the same year. (G. W. Sharpe)

140) BR Class 9F 2-10-0 No 92249 throws a blanket of smoke into the Fells as it labours up Shap on a mixed freight, with rear end assistance on 28th September 1967. (B. J. Miller)

141) SR Rebuilt *Battle of Britain* Class 4-6-2 No 34056 *Croydon* looks rather majestic outside 70E Salisbury shed on 5th February 1967. Despite its good external condition *Croydon* was to be withdrawn three months later. Salisbury continued to service steam until July 1967. (G. W. Sharpe)

142)   LMS Class 8F 2-8-0 No 48473 exudes a lazy pall of black smoke from its chimney whilst at rest in the shed yard at 55D Royston on 19th March 1967. Royston closed to steam in November 1967. (A. Wakefield)

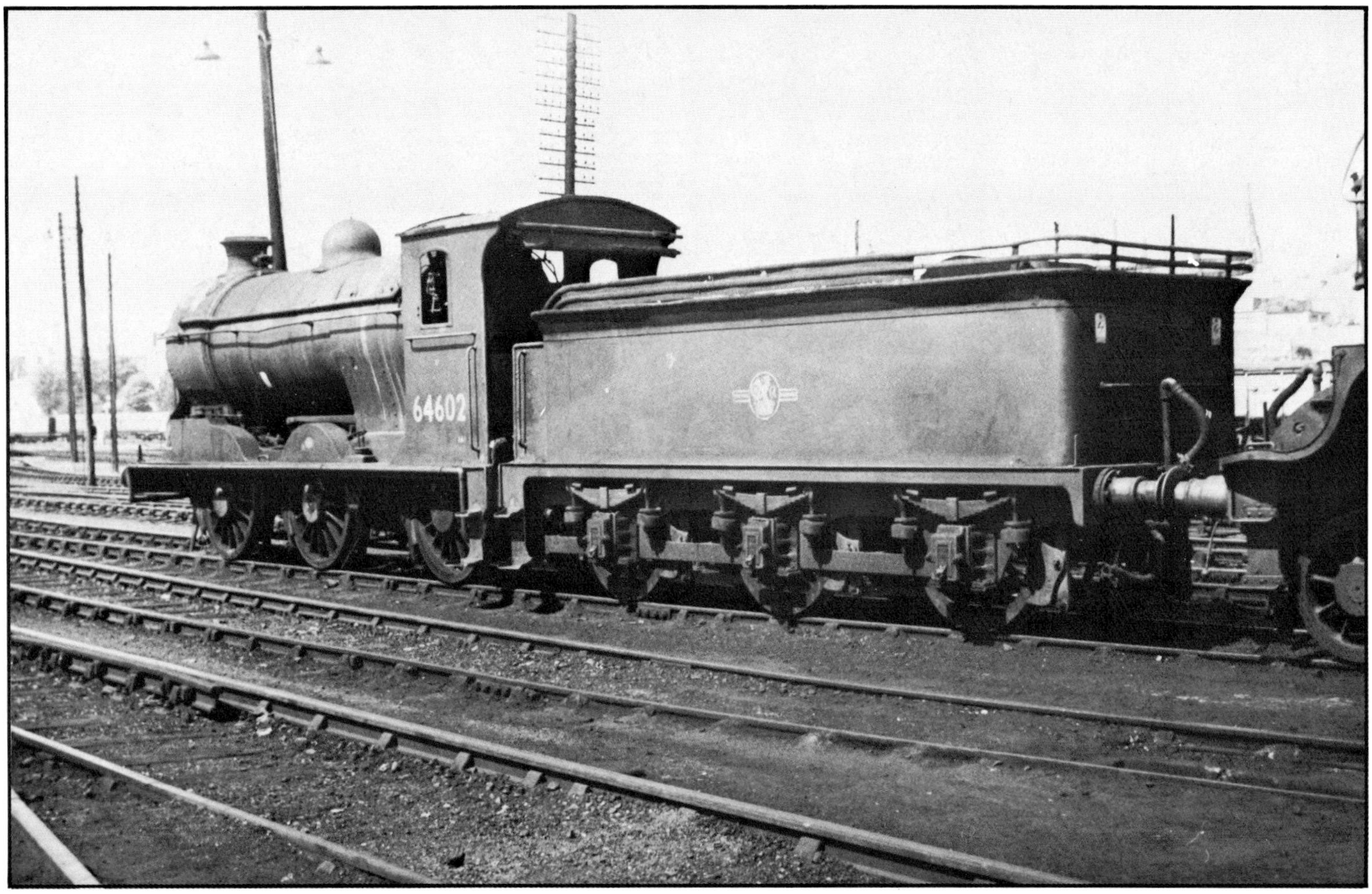

143)   LNER Class J37 0-6-0 No 64602 withdrawn and minus motion stands in store at 62B Dundee Tay Bridge and waits for its last journey to Motherwell for scrapping – 10th July 1967. (S. Turnbull)

144)   LMS Class 5 4-6-0 No 45395 at Greetland in the Calder Valley with an express during the summer of 1967. (G. W. Sharpe)

145)   BR *Britannia* Class 4-6-2 No 70023 *Venus* passes Carlisle (Kingmoor) shed on 11th June 1967 with a Glasgow-Crewe mail train. The diesel depot being constructed on the left was to be the death-knell of steam in the Carlisle area. (N. E. Preedy)

146) Eastleigh shed is almost deserted as is the yard, photographed from the footplate of a withdrawn SR Rebuilt *West Country* Class 4-6-2 in April 1967. The shed remained open until the end of Southern steam in early July 1967. (A. Dart)

147) LMS *Jubilee* Class 4-6-0 No 45562 *Alberta* in immaculate condition is photographed at Carnforth on 7th October 1967 with the *South Yorkshireman* from Bradford-Carlisle. At one time it was rumoured that *Alberta* was earmarked for preservation but this was not to be as she was withdrawn in November 1967 and scrapped in May 1968. (N. E. Preedy)

148)   LMS Class 5 4-6-0 No 45428 prepares to depart from Huddersfield on 10th June 1967 with an SLS/MLS special. 45428 was taken out of service in October 1967 and is preserved on the North Yorkshire Railway. (M. S. Stokes)

149)   The crew of SR Rebuilt *Battle of Britain* Class 4-6-2 No 34052 *Lord Dowding* are deep in conversation on a rainy and cold 20th January 1967 at Basingstoke. The express is the 11.30am Waterloo-Bournemouth. (W. G. Piggott)

150) BR Class 9F 2-10-0 No 92203 is utilised for passenger duty at Birkenhead on 5th March 1967 to mark the end of through workings from Paddington-Birkenhead. 92203 is preserved at Cranmore on the East Somerset Railway. (B. J. Miller)

151) LMS Class 5 4-6-0 No 44766 equipped with a double chimney storms out of Preston with the 16.20pm express from Crewe-Carlisle on 5th August 1967. (N. E. Preedy)

152) This relaxed onlooker has time on his side which is more than can be said about the row of redundant SR 02 Class
0-4-4 Tanks in store at Newport I.O.W. The locomotive in the centre can be identified as No 14 *Fishbourne*
photographed on 4th February 1967. A total of nine such engines were in store and all were scrapped by May 1967.
(D. Titheridge)

153) BR *Britannia* Class 4-6-2 No 70013 *Oliver Cromwell* at 12A Carlisle (Kingmoor) is prepared for special duty on 15th
October 1967. *Oliver Cromwell* survived in service until August 1968 and is preserved at Bressingham. (N. E. Preedy)

154)	The fireman of BR Class 4 4-6-0 No 75074 attempts to sort out a somewhat overloaded tender as the locomotive rests on the turntable at 70A Nine Elms shed on 14th April 1967. (W. G. Piggott)

155)	LMS Class 0F 0-4-0ST No 47005 in store at Rotherham in March 1967 prior to being scrapped the following month. (K. Shipley)

156)	The pioneer *Flying Pig* LMS Class 4 2-6-0 No 43000 in steam in the shed yard at 52F North Blyth on 13th July 1967. 43000 was withdrawn two months later and the shed closed at the same time. (R. Picton)

157)	BR Class 9F 2-10-0 No 92071 has a good head of steam after taking refreshment at Huddersfield in April 1967 whilst in charge of a tanker train. (G. W. Sharpe)

CHAPTER NINE – 1968

158)   BR Class 5 4-6-0 No 73050 lurks amidst the shadows inside 9H Patricroft shed on 12th May 1968. Patricroft consisted of two separate buildings and closed completely on 1st July 1968. No 73050 is preserved on the Nene Valley Railway. (P. B. Hands)

159) A trio of immaculate Class 5 4-6-0's the centre one being No 44888 are lined up outside 10D Lostock Hall shed on 4th August 1968. They and other locomotives had been specially cleaned to work enthusiasts excursions during steam's final hours. (A. C. Ingram)

160) The last surviving BR *Britannia* Class 4-6-2 No 70013 *Oliver Cromwell* was very much in demand for enthusiasts specials during 1968 and is the subject of admiration at Manchester (Victoria) on 28th July 1968. (R. Picton)

161)   In the latter months of steam, varied subject material was hard to find leaving the photographer little choice. Amongst the majority of surviving steam classes were the ubiquitous LMS Stanier Class 5 4-6-0's. One of their number 44949 is shown at Manchester (Victoria) during May 1968 after assisting an ailing EE Type 4 diesel with an express. (A. C. Ingram)

162)   The interior of 9H Patricroft shed is devoid of steam and smoke as the lifeless forms of BR Class 5 4-6-0 No 73133, an unidentified LMS Class 8F 2-8-0 and LMS Class 5 4-6-0 No 45187 are captured by the camera on 3rd June 1968. (C. P. Stacey)

163) Two surviving LMS Class 5 4-6-0's Nos 45110 and 45290 face the interior of 9K Bolton on 15th April 1968. Their immediate futures were to be entirely different with 45290 being withdrawn in June 1968 and scrapped but 45110 lasted until August 1968 and is preserved on the Severn Valley Railway. (R. Picton)

164) LMS Class 5 4-6-0 No 44891 on a centre road at Manchester (Victoria) in May 1968. The tender is adorned with various comments and judging by the size of the lumps of coal the fireman will be having his work cut out during the day. (A. C. Ingram)

165)   LMS Class 8F 2-8-0 No 48375 is in disguise as an 0-8-0 after collision damage at 10F Rose Grove on 16th March 1968. Needless to say 48375 was withdrawn and was so badly damaged it was cut up on site. Rose Grove was the last of three sheds to house steam and closed in August 1968. (G. W. Sharpe)

166)   LMS Class 5 4-6-0 No 44713 storms away from Carnforth on a rain-soaked 22nd June 1968 and heads for Barrow with a short parcels train. (P. B. Hands)

167) LMS Class 5 4-6-0 No 45318 from Bolton shed stands in the sidings at Mirfield with a rake of mineral wagons on a murky June day in 1968. Despite the loss of allocated steam engines on the North Eastern Region in November 1967 ex. LMS and BR classes continued to find their way on to this region almost to the end of steam. (G. W. Sharpe)

168) BR Class 4 4-6-0 No 75009 freshly withdrawn from service stands alone in a siding at 10A Carnforth on 4th August 1968. Along with Lostock Hall and Rose Grove, Carnforth was one of the last three depots to house working steam and is a working museum today. (W. G. Piggott)

169) Two fortunate locomotives both destined for preservation are in steam in the shed yard at 10D Lostock Hall on 4th August 1968. LMS Class 5 4-6-0 No 45110 (Severn Valley Railway) and BR *Britannia* Class 4-6-2 No 70013 *Oliver Cromwell* (Bressingham). (W. G. Piggott)

170) A grimy LMS Class 5 4-6-0 No 45202 from Newton Heath shed stands at Manchester (Victoria) station with a mail coach in May 1968. Newton Heath shed closed to steam on 1st July 1968. (A. C. Ingram)

171) BR Class 5 4-6-0 No 73069 departs from Earlstown with an enthusiasts special on 23rd June 1968. Based at Patricroft 73069 was transferred to 10A Carnforth upon the closure of the former depot on 1st July 1968 and became the last surviving working member of the class being withdrawn in August 1968. (B. J. Miller)

172) LMS Class 5 4-6-0 No 44889 in store at 10A Carnforth on 5th April 1968. Withdrawn in January 1968 44889 lingered at Carnforth for five months and was scrapped at Cohens, Kettering in June 1968. (R. Picton)

CHAPTER TEN – SCRAPYARDS

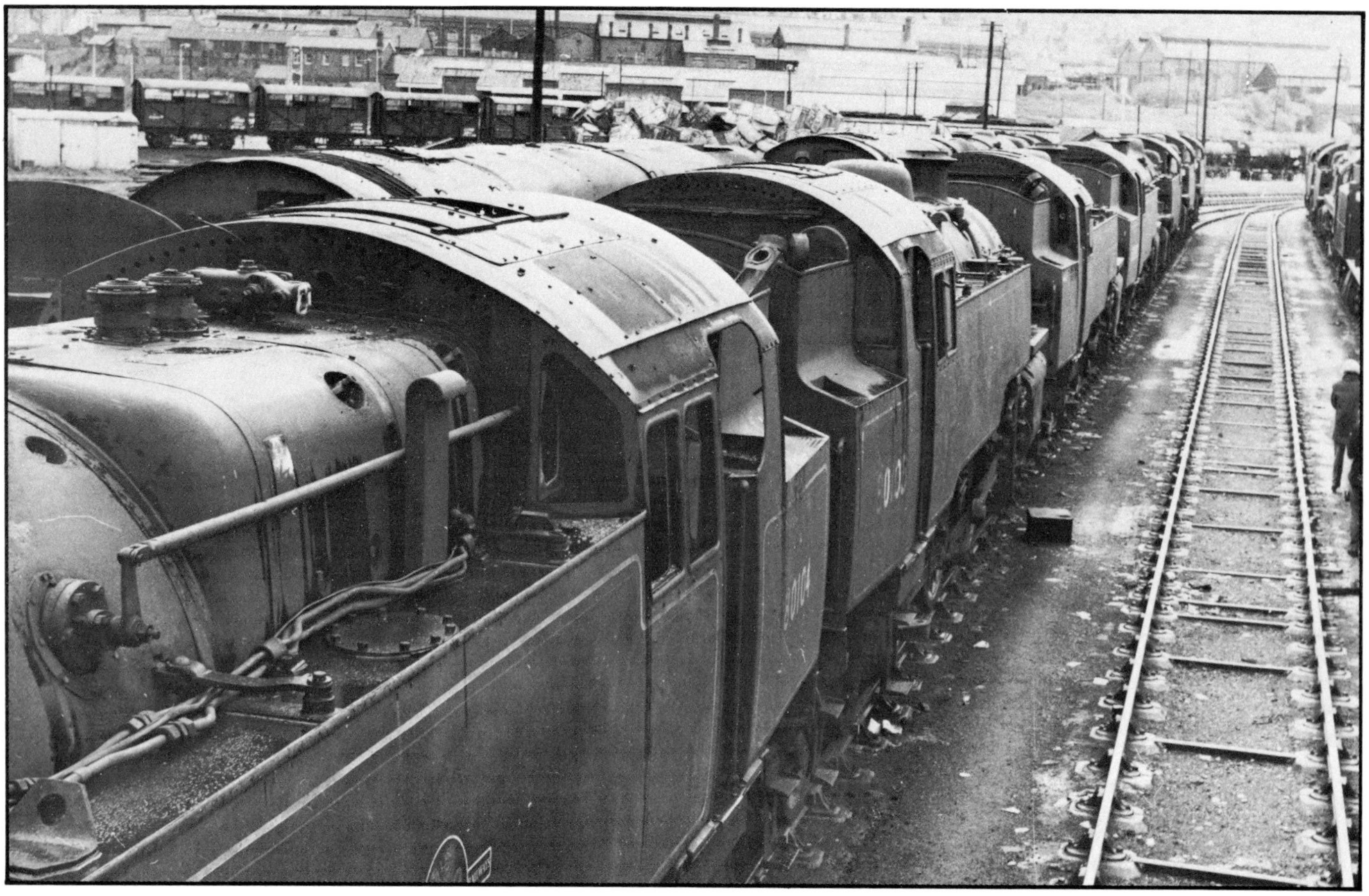

173) A row of condemned BR Class 4 2-6-4 Tanks contemplate a bleak future at Woodhams, Barry on 9th May 1966. Until the middle of 1962 all of these locomotives Nos 80104, 80105, 80098, 80097, 80080, 80079 and 80135 were active on the London Tilbury and Southend lines. However, thanks to the preservation movement all of these engines will be preserved. (A. Wakefield)

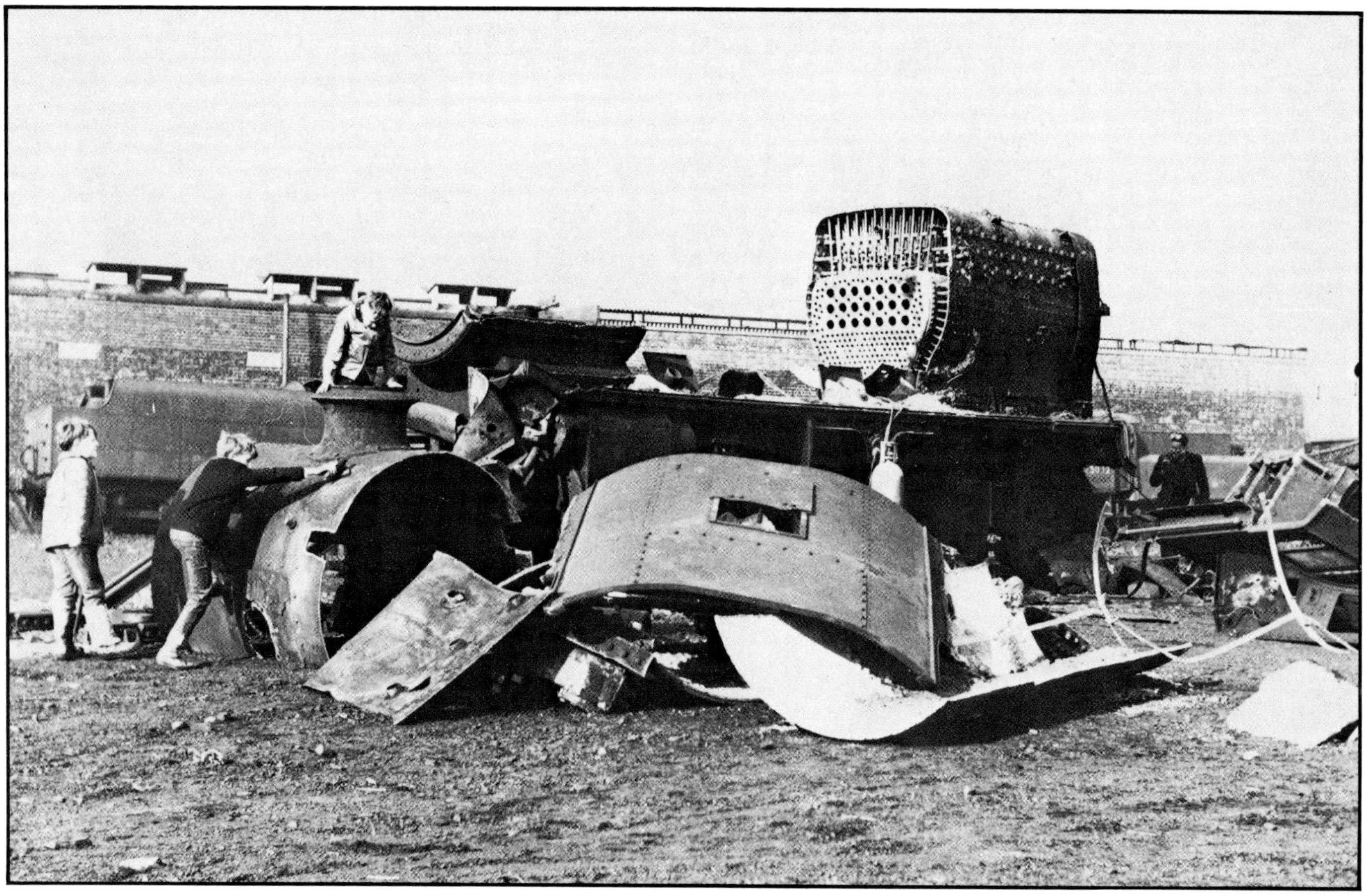

174) A group of children play amongst the remains of LMS Class 8F 2-8-0 No 48375 in the process of being cut up at 10F Rose Grove on 11th April 1968. This same engine is the subject of photograph No 165 on Page 90. (W. G. Piggott)

175) Cutting up has not long commenced as only the cab of LMS Class 6P5F 2-6-0 No 42830 has disappeared on 27th
March 1964 at Cowlairs Works. 42830 had been withdrawn in November 1962 and was stored for a long time at
Carlisle (Kingmoor) and Eastfield (Glasgow) before arriving at Cowlairs for scrapping. (B. Rands)

176) SR *King Arthur* Class 4-6-0 No 30739 *King Leodegrance* is being reduced to a shell by the cutters torch at Eastleigh
Works during May 1957. Note that the locomotive still has its right hand nameplate which presumably was cut up
with the engine. (T. Wright)

CHAPTER ELEVEN – PRESERVED LOCOMOTIVES

177) LNER K4 Class 2-6-0 No 3442 (ex. BR 61994) *The Great Marquess* and LNER Class N7 0-6-2T No 69621 repose in the silent roundhouse at 55H Leeds (Neville Hill) on 16th June 1968. *The Great Marquess* is preserved on the Severn Valley Railway and 69621 on the Stour Valley Railway. (P. B. Hands)

178) LMS *Royal Scot* Class 4-6-0 No 46115 *Scots Guardsman* minus nameplates languishes in store at 12A Carlisle (Kingmoor) on 14th July 1966. *Scots Guardsman* was the last member of the illustrious class to remain in service and was withdrawn in December 1965 – preserved at Dinting. (C. P. Stacey)

179) SR built *Merchant Navy* Class 4-6-2 No 35028 *Clan Line* nears completion of an extensive four year overhaul at her home base – Bulmers Railway Centre, Hereford on 24th September 1983. (J. D. Gomersall)